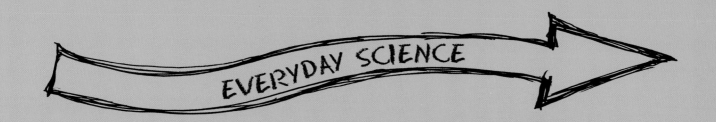
EVERYDAY SCIENCE

Materials

Please visit our web site at: www.garethstevens.com
For a free color catalog describing Gareth Stevens Publishing's list of high-quality books and multimedia programs, call 1-800-542-2595 or fax your request to (414) 332-3567.

Library of Congress Cataloging-In-Publication Data

Riley, Peter D.
    Materials / by Peter Riley. — North American ed.
      p. cm. — (Everyday science)
    Summary: An introduction to various types of materials and their different properties.
    Includes bibliographical references and index.
    ISBN 0-8368-3251-5 (lib. bdg.)
    1. Materials—Juvenile literature. [1. Materials.] I. Title.
    TA403.2.R55   2002
    620.1'1—dc21   2002022638

This North American edition first published in 2002 by
Gareth Stevens Publishing
A World Almanac Education Group Company
330 West Olive Street, Suite 100
Milwaukee, Wisconsin 53212 USA

Original text © 2001 by Peter Riley. Images © 2001 by Franklin Watts.
First published in 2001 by Franklin Watts, 96 Leonard Street, London, EC2A 4XD, England.
This U.S. edition © 2002 by Gareth Stevens, Inc.

Series Editor: Rachel Cooke
Designers: Jason Anscomb, Michael Leamen Design Partnership
Photography: Ray Moller (unless otherwise credited)
Gareth Stevens Editor: Mary Dykstra

Picture Credits: Ace Photo Agency/Martin Lipscombe, p. 13 (r); Alexis Sofianopoulos, p. 24 (l); Corbis Images, p. 25 (b and c);
Image Bank/Inner Light, p. 7; Pictor International, p. 24 (c); The Stock Market/Lester Lefkowitz, pp. 24 (r) and 25 (t).

The original publisher thanks the following children for modeling for this book: Jordon Conn, Nicola Freeman, Charley Gibbens,
Alex Jordan, Eddie Lengthorn, Henry Moller, and Rachael Moodley.

Printed in Hong Kong

1 2 3 4 5 6 7 8 9 06 05 04 03 02

EVERYDAY SCIENCE

Materials

Written by Peter Riley

Gareth Stevens Publishing
A WORLD ALMANAC EDUCATION GROUP COMPANY

About This Book

Everyday Science is designed to encourage children to think about their everyday world in a scientific way, by examining cause and effect through close observation and discussing what they have seen. Here are some tips to help you get the most from **Materials**.

- This book introduces the basic concepts of different materials and some of the vocabulary associated with them, such as transparent, waterproof, and the comparison of rough and smooth, and it prepares children for more advanced learning about materials.

- On page 15, children are asked to predict the results of a particular action. Be sure to discuss the reasons for any answers they give before turning the page. Giving reasons for answers is important, even if the answers are wrong. Set up other activities for the children and discuss possible outcomes.

- Be sure that children understand the difference between an object and the material from which it is made. Help them collect materials, such as wood or rock, that have not been shaped into objects.

- Further develop the information about senses on pages 10 and 11. For example, put a collection of objects into a drawstring bag. Ask children to describe the materials, just by touching them, using words from the book, such as hard or soft.

- Use the activity and the table on pages 26 and 27 to discuss the advantages of making an object out of more than one kind of material.

Contents

Different Materials

There are many kinds of materials.

This T-shirt is made of acrylic. Acrylic is a type of plastic.

These pants are made of cotton.

These shoes are made of leather.

6

This drainpipe is made of plastic.

This window is made of glass.

This door is made of wood.

This wall is made of brick.

Plastic, cotton, leather, glass, wood, and brick are materials.

7

Objects and Materials

One kind of material can be used to make very different objects. All of these objects are made of plastic.

brush

bottle

toothbrush

fork

All of these
objects are
made of metal.

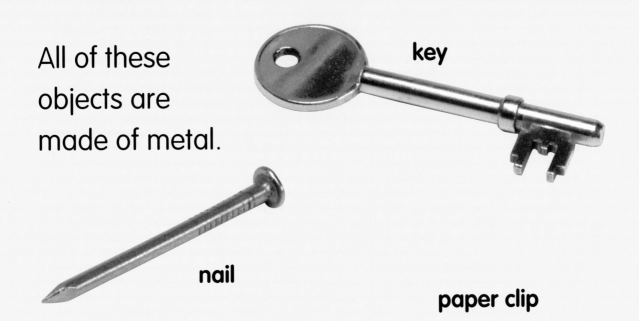

key

nail

paper clip

baking pan

Using Our **Senses**

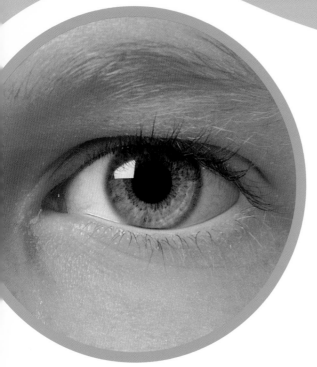

We use our senses to learn about the materials around us.

Our eyes see the colors of materials.

This wood is brown.

This brick is red.

This rock is gray.

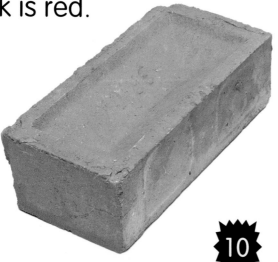

Our skin tells us how materials feel.

This rock feels rough.

This apple
feels smooth.

Color, roughness, and smoothness
are properties of materials.

What properties do your clothes have?

Hard or Soft

Hardness and softness are properties of materials, too.

metal

wool

wood

cotton

Nadia is going to sort these materials into a hard group and a soft group.

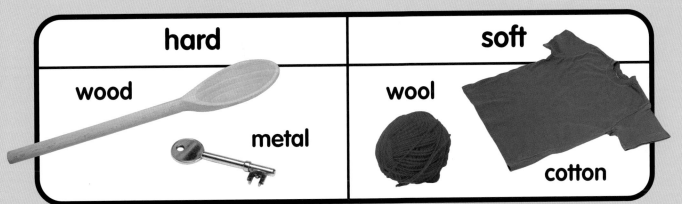

hard		soft	
wood	**metal**	**wool**	**cotton**

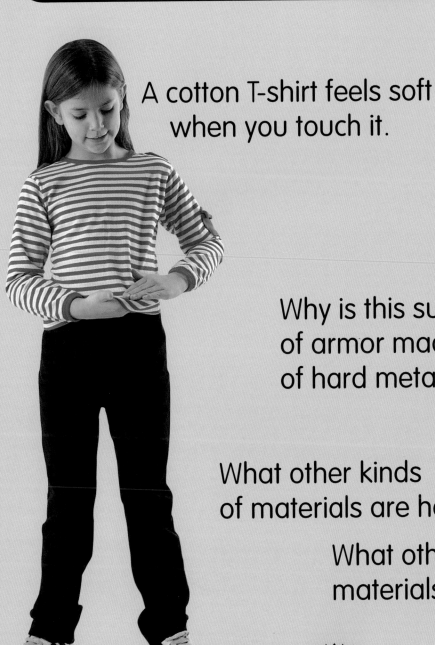

A cotton T-shirt feels soft when you touch it.

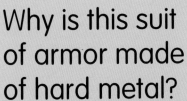

Why is this suit of armor made of hard metal?

What other kinds of materials are hard?

What other kinds of materials are soft?

Rough or Smooth

Materials can be rough or smooth.

Rough materials feel bumpy and uneven. A rough scouring pad cleans off dirt.

Smooth materials feel flat and even. Rain runs right off the smooth surface of an umbrella.

Toby is going to sort these six different materials into groups.

He will make a rough group and a smooth group.

plastic

sandpaper

cardboard

metal

glass

clay

Where will he put each kind of material?
Turn the page to find out.

Sorting Materials

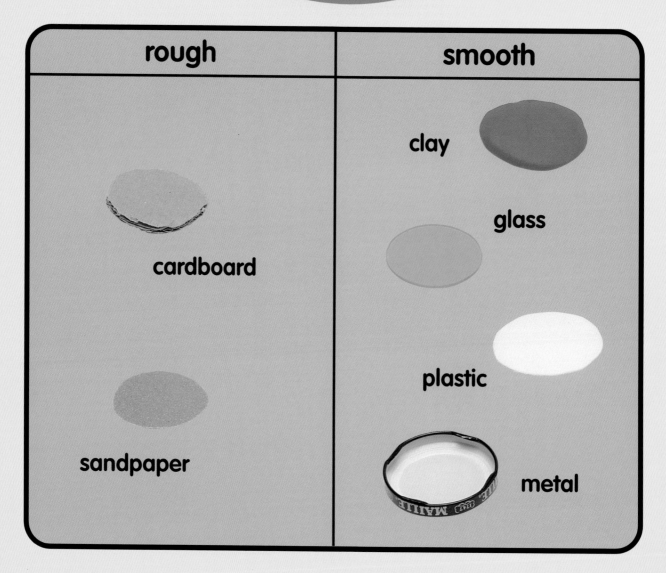

rough	smooth
cardboard	clay
sandpaper	glass
	plastic
	metal

Sort these materials again.
Put materials that can bend into a bendable group.
Put materials that cannot bend into a rigid group.

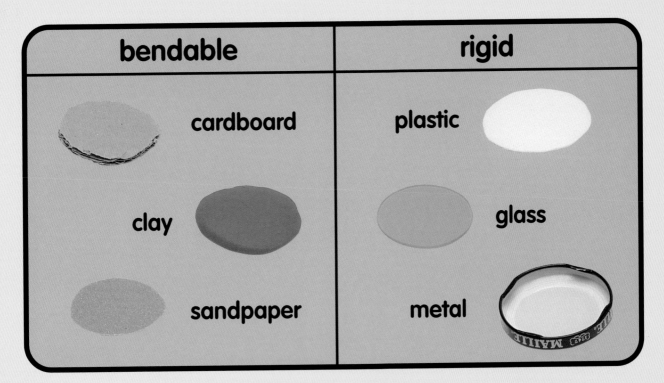

bendable	rigid
cardboard	plastic
clay	glass
sandpaper	metal

Plastic bags
are flexible,
or bendable.

Plastic pens are rigid.
They cannot bend.

Plastic can be either
flexible or rigid.
Can metal be either
flexible or rigid?

Will It  Stretch?

Some materials can stretch.
Other materials cannot stretch.

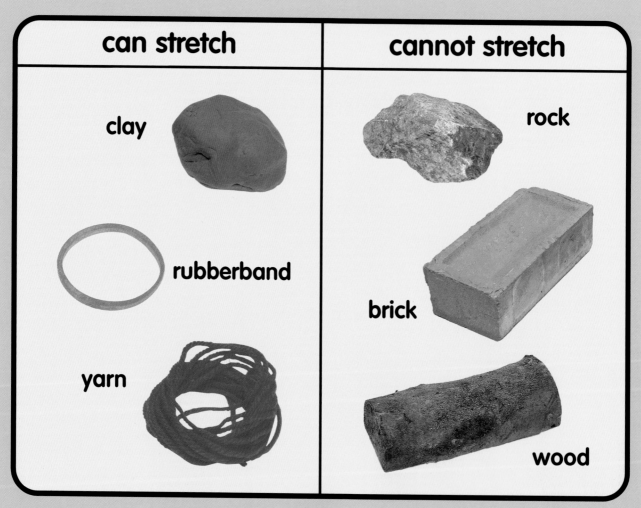

can stretch	cannot stretch
clay	rock
rubberband	brick
yarn	wood

Some hats are
made of wool.

A wool hat
stretches to
fit your head.

Can you think of other
reasons why wool is
a good material for
making hats?

Why aren't hats
made of brick?

See  Through This!

Materials can be opaque or transparent.

Brick, wool, and wood are opaque materials. You cannot see through them.

Most of the materials clothes are made of are opaque.

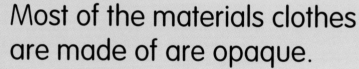

Plastic wrap and glass are transparent materials. You can see through them.

Glass is used to make windows.

A glass
window lets
you see outside.

A glass
window also
lets in light from
outside so you
can see inside.

What other property does glass have that
makes it a good material for windows?
Turn the page to find out.

Waterproof Materials

Glass is waterproof.

It does not let water pass through it.

A glass window keeps rain out.

Find some more waterproof materials with this test.

1. Cover a table with paper.

2. Place six different kinds of materials on the paper. Jamal is using plastic, glass, cardboard, metal, cotton, and paper.

3. Drop some water onto each material.

4. Wait five minutes, then look at each material. Can you still see the water? Now look underneath each material. Is the paper on the table wet?

The paper is dry under the plastic, glass, cardboard, and metal. It is wet under the cotton and paper.

Which materials are waterproof?

Natural or Made

Some materials come from nature. They are called natural materials. Other materials are made by people. They are called "made" materials.

People use natural materials to make many useful objects. Wood, wool, and clay are natural materials.

24

People mix natural materials to make new materials. The new materials are "made."

Paper is made by mixing wood with other materials.

Glass is made from sand and certain types of rock.

Plastic is made from oil that is found in the ground.

Plastic can be molded into many different shapes.

Material  Hunt

Gather some different objects from around the room.

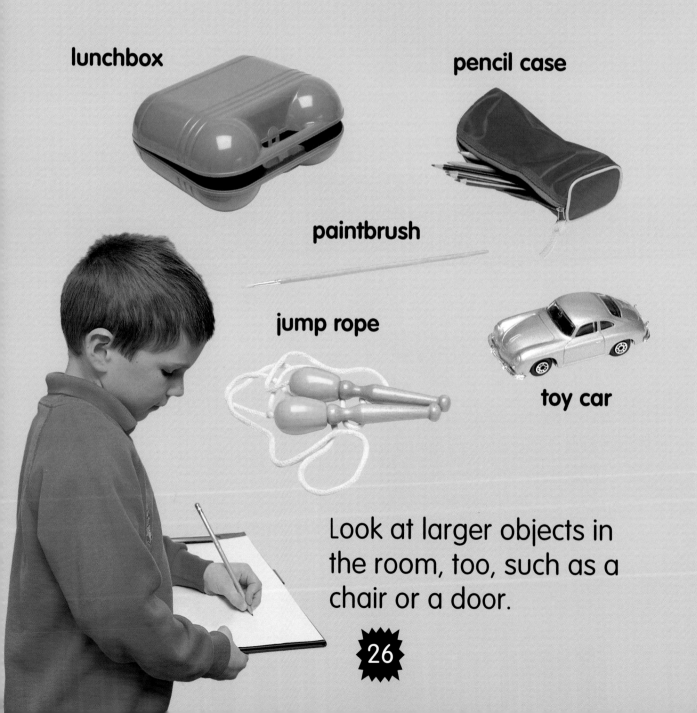

lunchbox

pencil case

paintbrush

jump rope

toy car

Look at larger objects in the room, too, such as a chair or a door.

Decide what kind of material each object is made of. Make a chart like this one to record the materials and the properties for each object.

	fabric	glass	paper	plastic	metal	wood	properties
lunch-box				✓			hard and smooth
jump rope	✓					✓	flexible/hard and smooth
paint-brush				✓	✓	✓	flexible/rigid
pencil case				✓	✓		flexible/hard and smooth
toy car				✓	✓		hard and smooth
chair	✓					✓	?
door		✓				✓	?

Are most of the objects you listed made of more than one material?

What properties do a chair and a door have?

Useful Words

fabric: a material that is made by weaving fibers, or threads, together. The cotton cloth a shirt is made of is fabric.

flexible: bendable, not rigid. Wool is a flexible material.

"made" material: a material that is created by people, usually in a factory and often by mixing natural materials together.

natural material: a material that comes from nature.

opaque: not see-through or transparent. Wood is an opaque material.

properties: the characteristics of a material that help us describe that material. One kind of material can have many different properties. Glass, for example, is hard and smooth and transparent.

rigid: stiff, not bendable. Brick and glass are rigid materials.

senses: the special abilities of the human body to hear, see, smell, taste, and touch.

transparent: see-through or clear. Glass is a transparent material.

waterproof: not letting water pass through. An umbrella is made of waterproof fabric.

Some Answers

Here are some answers to the questions asked in this book. If you had different answers, you may be right, too. Talk over your answers with other people and see if you can explain why they are right.

page 11 This answer depends on the clothes you are wearing. What colors are they? Are they soft? Do they keep you warm? Look at their labels to see what kinds of materials they are made of.

page 13 A suit of armor is made of hard metal so it will protect the soldier inside. Hard materials include rock, brick, glass, and some types of plastic. Soft materials include unbaked clay, wool, silk, and tissue paper.

page 17 Like plastic, some metal is flexible, and some is rigid. Aluminum foil is flexible, but a steel bowl is rigid. Sometimes, a metal object, such as a fork, is rigid, but it will bend if you are strong enough!

page 19 Wool is a good material for making hats because it is soft, and it is warm. Hats are not made of brick because brick is hard and heavy, and it cannot stretch to fit your head.

page 23 The plastic, glass, cardboard, and metal kept the paper dry. They are waterproof. In our test, the water on the cardboard seemed to disappear. It soaked into the cardboard. Do you think that cardboard is always waterproof? The thickness of a material often determines whether it is waterproof or not.

page 27 Since so many objects are made of more than one material, most of the objects on your list will probably have more than one material. The properties of a chair made of wood and fabric would include hard and rigid and soft and flexible. A door made of wood and glass would be hard and smooth.

For More Information

More Books to Read

- *Cotton Now & Then: Fabric-Making from Boll to Bolt.*
  Karen Bates Willing and Julie Bates Dock
  (Now & Then Publications)

- *Feeling Things. Rookie Read-About Science* (series)
  Allan Fowler
  (Children's Press)

- *What is it made of? Experiments in Science* (series)
  David Glover
  (Dorling Kindersley)

Web Sites

- Papermaking Process
  www.ppic.org.uk/htdocs/paper/process.htm

- ThinkQuest: Fabric Online
  library.thinkquest.org/C004179/textiles.html

Index